MUDRAS

for

VIRGO

By Sabrina Mesko Ph.D.H.

The material contained in this book has been written for informational purposes and is not intended as a substitute for medical advice nor is it intended to diagnose, treat, cure, or prevent disease. If you have a medical issue or illness, consult a qualified physician.

A Mudra Hands™ Book
Published by Mudra Hands Publishing

Copyright © 2013 Sabrina Mesko Ph.D.H.

Photography by Mara
Animal photography by Sabrina Mesko
Illustrations by Kiar Mesko
Cover photo by Mara

Printed in the United States of America

ISBN-13:978-0615920917
ISBN-10:0615920918

For all my Virgo Friends

TABLE OF CONTENTS

THE MUDRA PRACTICE IS A
COMPLIMENTARY HEALING TECHNIQUE,
THAT OFFERS FAST AND EFFECTIVE
POSITIVE RESULTS.

MUDRAS WORK HARMONIOUSLY
WITH OTHER TRADITIONAL,
ALTERNATIVE AND COMPLEMENTARY
HEALING PROTOCOLS.

THEY HELP RESTORE DEPLETED
SUBTLE ENERGY STATES
AND OPTIMIZE THE PRACTITIONER'S
OVERALL STATE OF WELLNESS.

Mudras for VIRGO

AUGUST 24 - SEPTEMBER 22

BODY
Nervous system, stomach, intestines

PLANET
Mercury

COLORS
Navy blue, dark brown, green

ELEMENT
Earth

STONES and GEMS
Sardonyx

ANIMAL
Domestic pets, dogs

Introduction

Ever since I can remember, I have been fascinated by the never ending view of the stars in the sky and the presence of other mysterious planets. As a child I wondered for hours about where does the Universe end and when my Father explained the possibility that time and space exist in a very different way than we imagined, my mind went wild with possibilities. I was however quite skeptical about astrology in general until one day in my early youth, a dear friend introduced me to a true Master of Vedic Astrology. He quickly and completely diminished any of my doubts about how precise certain facts can be revealed in one's Celestial map.

It was as if an invisible veil had been removed, and I was granted a peek over to the other side. The astrologer also adamantly pointed out that nothing is written in stone and one's destiny has a lot of space to navigate thru. You can make the best of the situation if you know your given parameters. My fascination and use of astrological science continues to this day and compliments and enriches my work with other observation techniques that I use when consulting.

One is born with character aspects and potential for realization of mapped-out future events, but there is always a possibility that another road may be taken. This has to do with the choices we make. Free will is given to all of us, even though often the choices we have seem to be very limited. But still, the choices are always there, forcing us to consciously participate and eventually take responsibility for our decisions, actions, and consequences.

The science of Astrology has been around for millenniums and even though some people are still doubtful, I always remind them that there is no disputing the fact, that the Moon affects the high and low tide of our Oceans - hence our bodies consisting mostly of water are affected by planetary movements in many fascinating and profound ways. Even the biggest skeptic agrees with that fact.

The Love of the Universal Power for each one of us is unconditional, everlasting and omnipresent. No matter what kind of life-journey you have, it is the very best one designed especially for you, rest assured. And when you are experiencing life's various challenges and wishing for a smooth ride instead, keep in mind that a life filled with lessons is a life fulfilling its purpose. The tests you encounter in your daily life are your opportunities.The wisdom learned is your asset, and the experiences gained are your wealth. Your Spirit's abundance is measured by the battles you fought and how you fought them. Did you help others and leave this world a better place in any way? Your true intention matters more than you know.

Each one of us has a very unique-one of a kind celestial map placed gently, but firmly and irrevocably into effect at the precise time of our birth. There are certain aspects of one's chart that reveal possible character tendencies and predisposed behavior in regards to love, partnerships, maintaining one's health, pursuit of success and a way of communicating. The benefits of knowing and understanding the effects of your chart on various aspects of your life can be profound. It can help you understand and prepare ahead of time for certain circumstances that are coming your way, which increases the possibility of a better quality of life in general.

If you knew that a specific time period could be beneficial for your career wouldn't it be good to know that ahead of your plans? If you are aware that certain aspects of your physical constitution are predisposed to a weakness or sensitivity, wouldn't it be beneficial to pay attention and prevent a possible future health ailment?

If you can foresee that a certain time will be slower for you in achieving positive results, wouldn't it be wise to use that time for preparation for a more fortuitous timing? How many times have you attempted to pursue a dream of yours that just didn't seem to want to happen? And when you were completely exhausted and disillusioned, the fortunate opportunity presented itself, except now you were tired, overwhelmed and had no energy or enthusiasm left. Having such information ahead of time would offer you the chance to save your energy during quiet, less active time, so that when your luck is more likely, you can seize the opportunity and make the most of it. Since writing my first books on Mudras a while ago, my work has expanded into many different areas, however I always included Mudras into my new ventures. When I designed International Wellness and Spa centers, I included Mudra programs to share these beneficial techniques with a wide audience. I included Mudras into my weekly TV show and guided large audiences thru practice on live shows.

Mudras will forever fascinate me and I have been humbled and excited how many practitioners from around the world have written me, grateful to have these techniques and most importantly really experiencing positive effects in time of need. Therefore it has been a natural idea for me to combine these two of my favorite topics and create a series of Mudra sets for all twelve Astrological signs.

The Mudras depicted in this book are specifically selected for the astrological sign of Aries with intention to help you maximize your gifts and soften the challenges that your celestial map contains.

It is important to know that each astrological chart - celestial map-contains information that can be used beneficially and there are no "bad signs" or "better sings". Your chart is unique as are you. By gaining information, knowledge and understanding what the placements of the planets offer you, your path to self knowledge is strengthened.

I hope this book will attract astrology readers as well as meditation and yoga practitioners and help you utilize the beneficial combination of both these fascinating techniques. Knowledge will help you experience the very best possible version of your life. The biggest mystery in your life is You. Discover who you are and enjoy the journey.

And remember, no matter what life presents you with, don't forget to smile and keep a happy heart. With each experience gained you are spiritually wealthier for it. And that my friend, stays with you forever.

The wisdom gained is eternally imprinted in your soul.

Blessings,

Sabrina

MUDRAS

Mudras are movements involving   only fingers, hands and arms. Mudras originated in ancient Egypt where they were practiced by high priests and priestesses in sacred rituals. Mudras can be found in every culture of the world. We all use Mudras in our everyday life when gesturing while communicating and when holding our hands in various intuitive positions. Mudras used in yoga practice offer great benefits and have a tremendously positive overall effect on our overall state of well-being. By connecting specific fingertips and your palms in various Mudra positions, you are directly affecting complex energy currents of your subtle energy body. As numerous energy currents run thru your brain centers, Mudras help stimulate specific areas for an overall state of emotional, physical and mental well being.

INSTRUCTIONS FOR MUDRA PRACTICE

YOUR BODY POSTURE
During the Mudra practice sit in an upright position with a straight spine, with both your feet on the ground or in a cross legged position. Comfort is essential so that you may practice undisturbed and focus on proper practice positions.

YOUR EYES
Keep your eyes closed and gently lightly lift the gaze above the horizon.

WHERE
For achieving best results of ideal Mudra practice it is essential that you find a peaceful place, without distractions. Once your Mudra practice is established,   you can practice Mudras anywhere.

WHEN
You may practice Mudras at any time. Best times for practice
are first thing in the morning and at bedtime. Avoid
practicing Mudras on a full stomach, and after a big meal wait
for an hour before practice.

HOW LONG
Each Mudra should be practiced for at least 3 minutes at a
time. Ideal practice is 3 Mudras for 3 minutes each with a
follow up short 3 minutes of complete stillness, peace and
meditation or reflection.

HOW OFTEN
You may practice Mudras every day. Explore various Mudras
by selecting a Mudra that fits your specific needs for any
given day.

Breath Control

Proper breathing is essential for optimal Mudra practice. There are
two main breathing techniques that can be used with your practice.

LONG DEEP SLOW BREATH
Slowly and deeply inhale thru your nose while relaxing and
expanding the area or your solar plexus and lower stomach. Exhale
thru the nose slowly while gently contracting the stomach area and
pulling your stomach in. Pace your breathing slowly and notice the
immediate calming effects. This breathing technique is appropriate
for relaxation, inducing calmness and peace.

BREATH OF FIRE
Inhale and exhale thru the nose at a much faster pace while
practicing the same concept of expanding navel area and
contracting with each exhalation. Unless otherwise noted Mudras
are generally practiced with the long slow breath.The breath of fire
has an energizing, recharging effect on body and is to be used only
when so noted.

Chakras

Along our spine, starting at the base and continuing up towards the top of your head, lie subtle energy centers-vortexes-called charkas, that have a powerful effect on the overall state of your health and well being.
The practice of Mudras profoundly affects the proper function of these energy centers and magnifies their power.

Our subtle energy body is highly sensitive to outside sensory stimuli of sound, aromas, visuals and outside electric currents that constantly surround us. Frequencies that permeate specific locations may attract or bother you. Perhaps you may feel eager to stay somewhere where the energy suits you and yet feel suffocated when the environment does not agree with you. We are all sensitive to energies, but some of us feel them more than others.

A positive blend of energies with another person can create a magnet-like effect, whereas another person's negative unharmonious subtle energy field subconsciously pushes you away.

By leading healthy lives and optimizing the proper function of charkas, you empower your subtle energy bodies adding strength to your physical body, mind and spirit. Destructive behavior like addictions and abuse weakens your Auric field and "leaks" your vital energy. By maintaining a healthy Aura-energy field, you can fine-tune your natural capacity for "sensing" places, situations and people that compliment your energy frequency.
In a state of "clean energy" you achieve capacity for high awareness and become your own best guide.

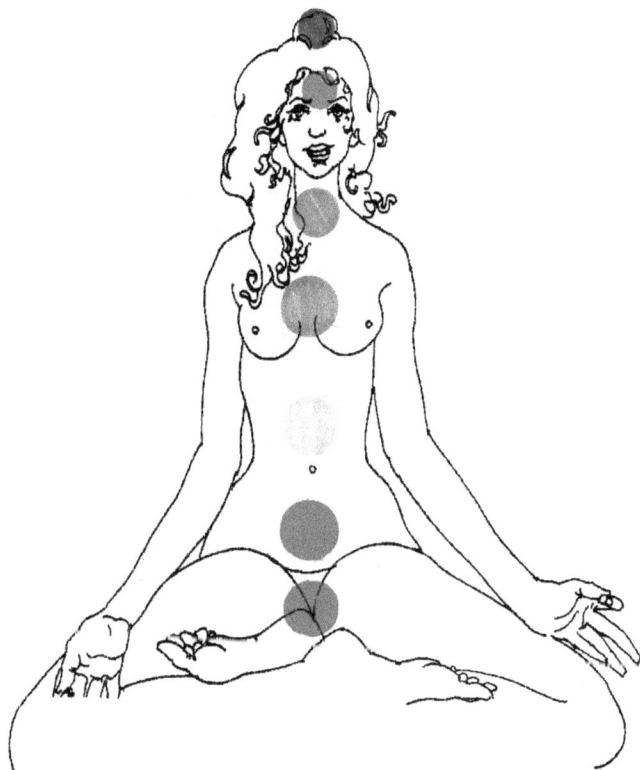

CHAKRAS IN THE BODY

Base Chakra: Foundation
Second Chakra: Sexuality
Third Chakra: Ego
Fourth Chakra: Love
Fifth Chakra: Truth
Sixth Chakra: Intuition
Seventh Chakra: Divine Wisdom

FIRST CHAKRA
LOCATION: Base of the spine
GLAND: Gonad
COLOR: Red
REPRESENTS:
Foundation, shelter, survival,
courage, inner security, vitality

SECOND CHAKRA
LOCATION: Sex organs
GLAND: Adrenal
COLOR: Orange
REPRESENTS:
Creative expression, sexuality,
procreation, family

THIRD CHAKRA
LOCATION: Solar plexus
GLAND: Pancreas
COLOR: Yellow
REPRESENTS:
Ego, intellect, emotions of fear and anger

FOURTH CHAKRA
LOCATION: Heart
GLAND: Thymus
COLOR: Green
REPRESENTS:
All matters of the heart, love,
self–love, compassion and faith

FIFTH CHAKRA
LOCATION: Throat
GLAND: Thyroid
COLOR: Blue
REPRESENTS:
Communication, truth,
higher knowledge, your voice

SIXTH CHAKRA
LOCATION: Third Eye
GLAND: Pineal
COLOR: Indigo
REPRESENTS:
Intuition, inner vision, the Third eye

SEVENTH CHAKRA
LOCATION: Top of the head - Crown
GLAND: Pituitary
COLOR: White and Violet
REPRESENTS:
The universal God consciousness,
the heavens, unity

NADIS

Your subtle energy body contains an amazing network of electric currents called Nadis. There are 72.000 energy currents that run throughout your body from toes to the top of your head as well as your fingertips. These channels of light must be clear and vibrant with life force for your optimal health and empowerment. With regular Mudra practice you can open, clear, reactivate and re-energize your energy currents.

Your Hands and Fingers

While practicing Mudras you are magnifying the effects of the Solar system on your physical, mental and spiritual body. Each finger is influenced by the following planets:

THE THUMB - MARS

THE INDEX FINGER - JUPITER

THE MIDDLE FINGER - SATURN

THE RING FINGER – THE SUN

THE LITTLE FINGER - MERCURY

MANTRA

Combining the Mudra practice with appropriate Mantras magnifies the beneficial effects of these ancient self-healing techniques.

The hard palate in your mouth has 58 energy meridian points that connect to and affect your entire body.

By singing, speaking or whispering Mantras, you touch these energy points in a specific order that is beneficial and has a harmonious and healing effect on your physical, mental and spiritual state.

The ancient science of Mantras helps you reactivate nadis, magnifies and empowers your energy field, improves your concentration and stills your mind.

About Astrology

The word Horoscope originates from a Latin word ORA–hour and SCOPOS–view. One could presume that Horoscope means "a look into your hour of birth". The precise moment of your birth determines your celestial set-up.

An accurate astrological chart can reveal most detailed aspects of your life, your character, your gifts, your future possible events, challenges that await you, lucky events that are bestowed upon you, and your outlook for happy relationships, successful careers, accomplishments, health and many possible variations of life events. I say possible, because your decisions will determine the outcome.

There are 12 signs in the Zodiac and your birth-day reflects the position of your Sun sign. The specific positions of other planets in your chart are calculated considering the precise moment-hour and minute and of course location of your birth. The birth time will reveal your Rising or Ascending sign, which will further determine other essential facts of your chart.

The constant transitional movements of the Planets affect each one of us differently, a time that may be difficult for some may prove supremely lucky for another and yet we are interconnected by mutual effects of continuous planetary movements. Nothing is standing still, the changes are ongoing. On a different note, a few slow moving planets connect us in other ways, as they keep certain generations under specific aspects and influences. We are all inseparable and in continuous motion.

There are numerous fascinating ways to use astrology and there is no doubt that the constant motion of all these powerful and majestic Planets in our Solar system affect each and every one of us differently. Astrology can be used as an additional tool to help you continue progressing on the mysterious life journey of self discovery and self-realization.

Remember, the power of decision is yours as is the responsibility for consequences. Make peace with your doubts, pursue your dreams and relish in results.

When the outcome is less than what you expected, learn to pick yourself up and continue on, wiser with knowledge you gained, that alone being a good reason for remaining optimistic. When the outcome surpasses your expectations, well, then you will know what to do…mostly take a breath, smile, and enjoy the moment.

YOUR SUN SIGN

There are 12 signs in the Zodiac. The day of your birth determines your Sun-sign. Most often this is the extent of average person's knowledge and interest in astrology. However, the other aspects in the astrological chart are equally as important and need to be taken into consideration. In this book your main guide is your Sun sign's dispositions, tendencies, weaknesses and gifts. Certainly there are endless combinations of charts and your Sun sign alone will not reveal the complete picture of your celestial map.

For more detailed information and reflection about your chart, you need to know your ascending-rising sign.

Your Ascending-Rising Sign

Your rising sign, also known as the ascendant, reflects the degree of ecliptic rising over the eastern horizon at the precise moment of your birth. It reveals the foundation of your personality. That means that even if you have the same birthday with someone else, your time of birth would create completely different aspects and influences in your chart. No two people are alike. You are one of a kind and so is everyone else. However, you may have some strong similarities and timing aspects that will be often alike. Your rising sign also reveals the basis of your chart and House placements. Your rising sign determines and is in your first house. There are 12 Houses and each depicts precise in-depth information about all aspects of your physical life, emotional make and character tendencies. It is incredibly complex and fascinating. Regarding your Mudra practice in combination with your Astrological Sign, it would be beneficial to know also your Rising sign and apply Mudras that empower your Rising sign as well. For example; if your Sun sign is VIRGO, but your rising sign is Libra-it would be most beneficial to practice Mudra sets for both signs.

How to use this book

In each book of the *Mudras for the Astrological Signs* series, you will find Mudras for different astrological signs that will help you in most important areas of your life: Health, Love, Success, and Overcoming your challenging qualities. We all have them, as we also all have gifts. This book is specific for the sign of Aries. You may change your Mudra practice daily as needed, and keep in mind, that certain habits or tendencies need a longer time to adjust, change, and improve. Be patient, kind, and loving towards yourself.

MUDRAS FOR TRANSCENDING CHALLENGES

Each one of us has a few character tendencies or weaknesses that are connected to our astrological chart. To help you transcend, overcome and redirect these challenges into your beneficial assets, you can use the Mudras in this chapter.

MUDRAS FOR HEALTH AND BEAUTY

Each astrological sign rules certain areas of your body. The Mudras in this chapter will help you strengthen your physical weaknesses while maintaining a healthy body, and a beautiful, vibrant appearance.

MUDRAS FOR LOVE

The Mudras in this chapter will help you understand your love temperament, your expectations, your longings and how to attract the optimal love partner into your life. It is most beneficial to know how others perceive you in the matters of the heart. It will also help you understand your partner and their astrologically influenced love map.

MUDRAS FOR SUCCESS

The Mudras in this chapter will offer you tools to present yourself to the world in your optimal light. Often one is confused in which direction to turn or where their strength lies. Mudras will help you focus and remember your essential creative desires, help you gain self-confidence and inner security to recognize your desired and destined path. If you know what you want, and your purpose is harmonious for the better good of all, your success is within reach.

MUDRAS
for TRANSCENDING
CHALLENGES

MUDRA for COMPASSION

Your great gift for details and your meticulous, reliable nature also creates a very high level of expectations. In other words- you are the ultimate perfectionist. You demand the best of yourself and others. Well, the reality is that sometimes these high expectations just can not be met. Your overly critical streak can take over and no one is happy, including you. To avoid succumbing to this characteristic, take a moment and truly "loosen up" the grip. See yourself in the position of the other person and open your heart to compassion and understanding. Nobody is perfect in this wold. The sooner you realize and accept that, the better for you and your level of contentment.

CHAKRA : 4

COLOR: Green

MANTRA:
AKAL AKAL SIRI AKAL
(Timeless Is the One Who Achieves
Perfection of the Spirit)

Sit with a straight spine. Extend your arms out to the sides parallel to the ground with the palms turned front. Stretch out the fingers and hold them still. Turn your head to the right side and back to the center four times, then to the left side and back to the center four times. Continue for a few minutes and concentrate on your heart center. Become aware of the energy in your palms.

BREATH: Inhale long once as you move your head to the right and exhale long once as you move your head back to center. Repeat four times to each side. Relax and sit still for a few minutes.

MUDRA for
RELEASING Negativity

Your intelligence, keen observation and analytical talents are true gifts that can bring you much success. However, it is possible that when not applied properly you could be seen as overly fussy and perhaps even harsh in your assessments. In order to deliver the information in the best possible format and successfully rely the message without a trace of negativity, this Mudra will be very helpful. Practice it before meetings or important exchanges so that your true gifts are recognized and not misunderstood, or met in a defensive manner. Transform your criticism into gentle but precise "redirecting" advice.

CHAKRA: 4

COLOR: Green

Sit with a straight back. Bend your arms and make fists with both hands. Bring them up in front of your heart. Cross the hands over each other, palms turned outwards. Hold the Mudra across the chest with the left arm on the outer side.

BREATH: Long, deep and slow.

MUDRA FOR RELAXATION AND JOY

After each successfully accomplished and completed project there needs to be a time of rest and relaxation. Enjoy the fruits of your labor and breathe. Of course it would be truly exceptional, if you were able to enjoy the entire process as well, for that is the point of life. Enjoying every step of the way and not just worrying about the end result or the final outcome. Every minute and day counts, so do not delay and practice this Mudra to help you remember how to live in the moment and feel carefree, joyful and happy each and every day.

CHAKRA : 3, 4

COLOR: Yellow, green

MANTRA:

HAREE HAR HAREE HAR
(God in His Creative Aspect)

Sit with a straight back, lift up your hands up in front of your chest. Make a fist with your left hand, tucking the thumb inside. Wrap the right hand around the left and place your right thumb over the base of the left thumb. Concentrate on your third Eye area and hold for three minutes. Later, extend your practice to eleven minutes.

BREATH: Long, deep and slow.

MUDRAS
for HEALTH
and BEAUTY

MUDRA FOR
SECOND CHAKRA

Your vulnerable area of stomach demands special attention and care. Every occasion that requires your extra strength and energy can show consequences and strain in that region. Pay close attention and find the ideal diet for you, always creating a peaceful environment when eating.   This Mudra will help you soothe, energize and protect that region so that you will overcome "nervous stomach" with ease and little effort.

CHAKRA : 2

COLOR: Orange

MANTRA:

SAT NAM
(Truth Is God's Name, One in Spirit)

Sit with a straight back. Place your left hand with palm facing down in front of your stomach area. Hold your right hand open, away from your body, the palm facing up.

BREATH: Long, deep and slow.

MUDRA FOR
STRONG NERVES

Your diligent and perfectionistic nature requires much patience and stamina. Your nervous system is put to a test and needs extra help and attention. That requires proper rest, a healthy diet, plenty of sleep, fresh air and generous time spend in nature. An overall holistic lifestyle and relaxation techniques are required. Mudras are ideal for you and it is most beneficial that you implement this practice into your daily life and make it a part of your required routine. This Mudra will help you maintain, preserve and protect your nerves. When you find yourself in any kind of stressful situations, take a few minutes to practice and feel immediate relief.

CHAKRA : 3, 4

COLOR: Yellow, green

Sit with a straight spine. Lift your left hand at ear level, palm facing out. Connect the thumb and middle finger and stretch out other fingers. Place your right hand in front of the solar plexus, palm facing up. The thumb and little finger are touching while other fingers are straight. **This position is reversed for men.**

BREATH: Long, deep and slow.

MUDRA FOR
RELEASING ANXIETY

All that worry and your fussy, analytical nature keeps you in a continuous state of suspense, expectation and under pressure. When things sway a bit into an unknown direction, your anxiety level rises and makes everything even more intense. With your many talents and abilities you are always automatically exposed to criticism and you being your own worst judge, this is not a recipe for peace and fun. However, help is on its way! This Mudra is extremely powerful and can transform you in a   matter of minutes into a serene and energetically empowered person that you want and deserve to be. Now you can be on your way and see your goals accomplished. Practice this Mudra every morning when a stressful day lies ahead and enjoy the beneficial, long lasting results.

CHAKRA : 4, 5, 6

COLOR: Green, blue, indigo, violet

MANTRA:
HARKANAM SAT NAM
(God's Name Is Truth)

Sit with a straight spine. Bend your elbows and raise your arms so your upper arms are parallel to the ground and extended out to the sides. Your hands are at the level of your ears, fingers spread wide and pointing to the sky. Start rotating your hands back and forth pivoting at the wrists. Practice for three minutes and be persistent. You will go thru a period when it seems difficult, but when you overcome that moment, the practice will be easy.

BREATH: Long, deep and slow.

MUDRAS
for LOVE

MUDRA FOR OPENING YOUR HEART

You are very demanding of yourself and entertain a harsh inner monologue. In order to attract a loving partner your way, who appreciates and generously unconditionally loves you, you need to love yourself truly unconditionally as well. That means when you see things about yourself that are not so perfect, make a decision to manage and overcome that tendency, and love yourself for who you are. This Mudra will help you open your heart and allow loving energy, people and situations to come your way. You can finally relax and be happy with who you are.

♍

CHAKRA : 4

COLOR: Green

MANTRA:
SAT NAM
(Truth is God's Name, One in Spirit)

Sit with a straight spine and lift your hands in front of your heart with palms and fingers open as if creating a cup. Keep all the fingers stretched and feel healing energy pouring into your fingertips and the area of your heart.

BREATH: Long, deep and slow.

MUDRA FOR LOVE

Once you fall in love, the main focus should be to truly enjoy the blissful times, and soak in every minute of happiness. You will do anything and everything for your partner, but you may forget to stop worrying or nagging about your imaginary imperfections. Your partner can not continuously assure you that you are great just the way you are, you need to truly embrace yourself and let go of any self-analyzing habit. Love is peace, harmony, togetherness, and calm soothing energy no matter where you are together. Just being you in enough. Practice this Mudra and consciously absorb the essence of love in every possible way.

CHAKRA : 4

COLOR: Green

MANTRA:
SAT NAM WAHE GURU
(God is Truth, His Is the Supreme Power
and Wisdom)

Sit with a straight spine and raise your hands to the either side of your head. Curl the middle and ring fingers into your palm an extend the thumbs, index fingers, and little fingers. Keep your elbows from sinking and hold for three minutes.

BREATH: Inhale for eight short inhalation counts, and exhale with one strong, long exhale.

MUDRA
FOR GUIDANCE

When you fall in love and open your heart to your lover, it is important to let go and truly let your mind have a rest. Not everything needs to be decided with your amazing mind. Matters of the heart need a different approach. You may not find it logical-the person whom you fall in love with-or even expected. Your dream partner may be completely different from what you imagined or thought it would be best. This is how love is; inexplicable and unpredictable. When you mind is trying to interfere with those wonderful moments of love, you need to practice this Mudra. It will help you learn how to hear your heart and engage in heartfelt guidance. Listen and just receive, no thinking required, just absolute stillness and receptivity. Give it a try. You will be amazed and transformed.

CHAKRA: 7

COLOR: White

Sit with a straight spine. Place your hands together in front of your chest. Little fingers are pressed together to form a cup. Palms are facing towards the sky. Leave a very small opening between the sides of the little fingers. Gently focus your eyes towards the tip of your nose towards the palms. Have a clear question. Hold for three minutes, relax, be calm and wait for a clear answer.

BREATH: Long, deep and slow into your palms.

MUDRAS for SUCCESS

MUDRA FOR
SELF - CONFIDENCE

Perfectionist that you are, your expectations of yourself are super high and unrealistic. This can be partially good because you will strive to be better and will be quite disciplined about your goals. But the other side of the coin is, that you may be to harsh on yourself. When you realize that your "norm" can not be met, you may have some confidence issues to fight with. They key is to relax these demands a bit and you will see that your very best is darn close to perfect anyway. To help you strengthen your confidence, practice this Mudra with dedication and intent. Redirect your mind patterns into a positive loving inner dialogue and affirmations. You are great just the way you are.

♍

CHAKRA : 3, 6

COLOR: Yellow, indigo

MANTRA:

EK ONG KAR SAT GURU PRASAD
SAT GURU PRASAD EK ONG KAR
(The Creator Is the One That Dispels Darkness
and Illuminates Us by Hs Grace)

Sit with a straight back. Lift your hands up to the level of your solar plexus with elbows bent to the sides. Bend the middle, ring, and little fingers and touch them back to back. Extend the index fingers and thumbs and press them together. The thumbs are pointed toward you and the index fingers away from you.

BREATH: Long, deep and slow.

MUDRA FOR CREATIVITY

When you amazing gifts of intelligence, practicality and perfectionism join, the results are achieved. The one element that needs to be implemented even more to truly produce a fulfilling new successful venture is your creativity. You need to tap into your core creative source and let your imagination fly. This Mudra will help you open up those channels and stimulate your creative energy so that what the project you work on truly surpasses everyone's imagination.

CHAKRA : 6, 7

COLOR: Indigo, violet

MANTRA:
GA DA
(God)

Sit with a straight spine. Connect the thumbs and index fingers, keeping the rest of the fingers straight. Bend your elbows and lift your hands to your sides with palms facing up at a sixty-degree angle to your body. Concentrate on your Third eye and meditate for at least three minutes.

BREATH: Short, fast, breath of fire from the navel.

MUDRA FOR
POWERFUL INSIGHT

Small details matter, but they are not most important all the time. Deciding what takes priority is needed to get the projects accomplished while seeing the big picture. Overworking a smaller issue takes you away from the main path. The hard worker that you are, it is essential that you make clear boundaries and are selective. Taking a moment and reflecting on priorities and dividing your workload is essential. This Mudra will help you come to a decision in this area and will assure that you have a healthy, but reasonable work tempo. Save your work energy for things that matter and are essential.

CHAKRA: 6

COLOR: Indigo

Sit with a straight back, elbows out to either side. Raise your hands until they meet above the navel point. The back of the left hand rests in the right palm and the thumbs are crossed, left over right.

BREATH: Long, deep and slow.

ABOUT THE AUTHOR

SABRINA MESKO **PH.D.H**. is an International and Los Angeles Times bestselling author of the timeless classic *Healing Mudras - Yoga for your Hands* translated into fourteen languages. She authored over twenty books on Mudras, Mudra Therapy, Mudras and Astrology, Holistic Caregiving, Spirituality and Meditation techniques.

Sabrina holds a Bachelors Degree in Sensory Approaches to Healing, a Masters in Holistic Science, a Doctorate in Ancient and Modern Approaches to Healing, and a Ph.D.H in Healtheoloyy from the American Institute of Holistic Theology. She is board certified from the American Alternative medical Association and American Holistic Health Association. She has been featured in media outlets such as The Los Angeles Times, CNBC News, Cosmopolitan, the cover of London Times Lifestyle, The Discovery Channel documentary on Hands, W magazine, First for Women, Health, Web-MD, Daily News, Focus, Yoga Journal, Australian Women's weekly, Blend, Daily Breeze, New Age, the Roseanne Show and various international live television programs. Her articles have been published in world-wide publications. She hosted her own weekly TV show educating about health, well-being and complementary medicine. She is an executive member of the World Yoga Council and has led numerous international Yoga Therapy educational programs. She directed and produced her interactive double DVD titled *Chakra Mudras* - a Visionary awards finalist.

Sabrina also created award winning international Spa and Wellness Centers and is a motivational keynote conference speaker addressing large audiences all over the world. She is the founder of Arnica Press, a boutique Book Publishing House. Her mission is to discover, mentor, nurture and publish unique authors with a meaningful message, that may otherwise not have an opportunity to be heard. She is the founder of world's only online Mudra Teacher and Mudra Therapy Education, Certification and Mentorship program, with her certified therapists spreading these ancient teachings in over 28 countries around the world.

www.SabrinaMesko.com

www.ingramcontent.com/pod-product-compliance
Lightning Source LLC
Chambersburg PA
CBHW071431040426
42445CB00012BA/1339